W9-BPR-976

# Georgia O'Keeffe

## Paintings

WINGS BOOKS
New York • Avenel, New Jersey

This 1994 edition is published by Wings Books, distributed by Random House Value Publishing, Inc., 40 Engelhard Avenue, Avenel, New Jersey 07001.

Random House
New York • Toronto • London • Sydney • Auckland

Printed and bound in Malaysia

**Library of Congress Cataloging-in-Publication Data**

O'Keeffe, Georgia, 1887–1986.
    Georgia O'Keeffe : paintings.
        p.   cm.
    Includes bibliographical references.
    ISBN 0-517-11923-4
    1. O'Keeffe, Georgia, 1887–1986—Catalogs.   I. Title.   II. Title:
Paintings.
ND237.05A4   1994
759.13—dc20                                                94-20417
                                                                CIP


8   7   6   5   4   3   2

*"I have picked flowers where I found them— Have picked up sea shells and rocks and pieces of wood. When I found the beautiful white bones in the desert I picked them up and took them home too. . . . I have used these things to say what is to me the wideness and wonder of the world as I live in it."*[1]

—GEORGIA O'KEEFFE

1.  *A Celebration*   1924

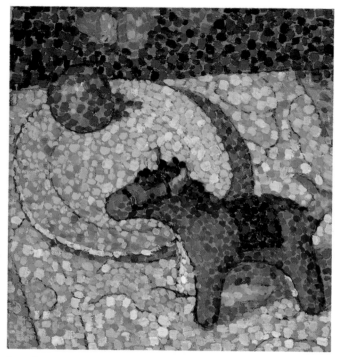

2. *Horse-Red* 1914

3.  *Evening Star No. VI*  1917

4.  *Alligator Pears in a Basket, No. 2*   1921

5.  *Apple Family III*   1921

6. *Corn, Dark II*   1924

7.  *Mountains and Lake*   1961

8.  *Abstraction, White Rose II*  1927

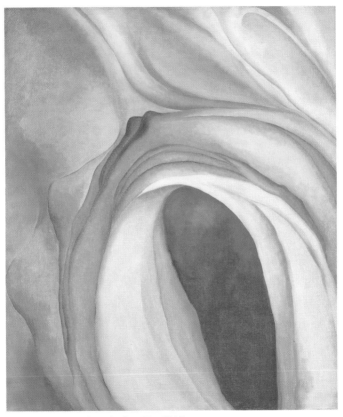

9.  *Music—Pink and Blue II*   1919

10. *Lake George Autumn* 1927

11.  *New York with Moon*  1925

12. *Patio Door with Green Leaf* 1956

13.  *Summer Days*  1936

14. *Hills and Mesa to the West*   1945

15.  *Ram's Head with Hollyhock*   1935

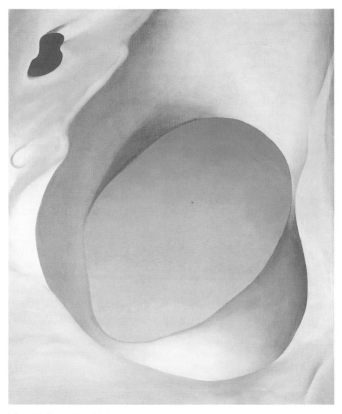

16. *Pelvis III* 1944

17. *Plums* 1920

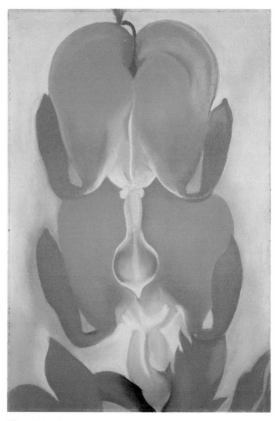

18.  *Bleeding Heart*   1932

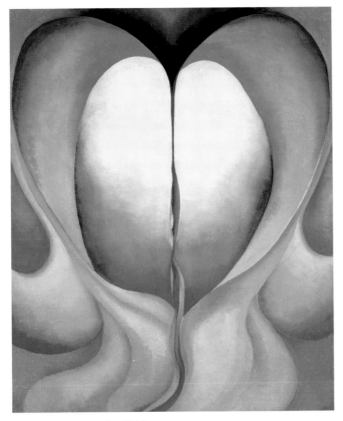

19. *Series I, No. 8*   1919

20. *The White Calico Flower* 1931

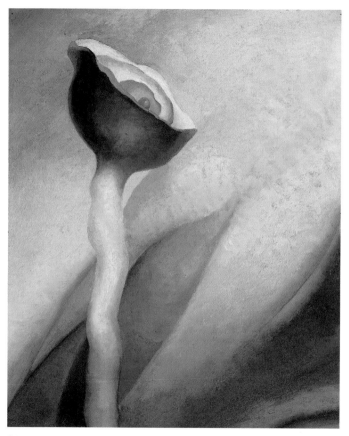

21.  *Series I, No. 2*  1918

22.  *Misti—A Memory*   1957

23. *Dry Waterfall* 1951

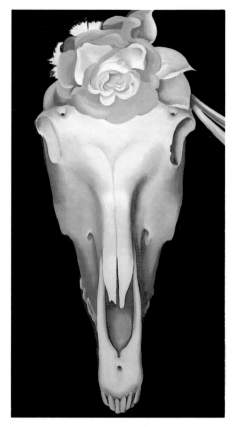

24.  *Horse's Skull with White Rose*   1931

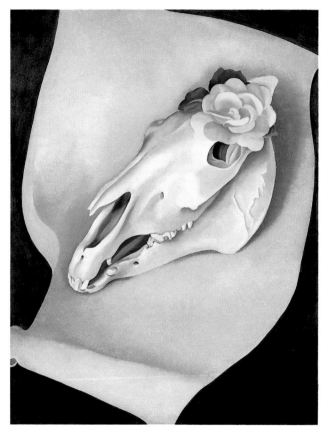

25.  *Horse's Skull with Pink Rose*    1931

26.  *White Iris*   1925

27.  *Pink Sweet Peas*   1927

28.  *The Broken Shell—Pink*   1937

29.  *Two Calla Lillies on Pink*    1928

30.   *Series I, No. 4*   1918

31.   *Goat's Horn with Red*   1945

32.   *Sky Above Clouds II*   1963

# Afterword

At the height of her career, Georgia O'Keeffe remarked, "Where I was born and where and how I have lived is unimportant. It is what I have done with where I have been that should be of interest."[2]

Where she had been was quintessential America: rolling farmlands in Wisconsin; tiny art studios and steel towers in Manhattan; vast open plains in Texas; summer lakes and shores in upstate New York; the limitless wash of sky and desert that is New Mexico. What she had *done* was see—through her mind's eye, through a studio window, at the juncture of sky and land, in the dirt at her feet, in a flower, a shell, a bone—the infinite possibilities inherent in illuminating nature in its pure organic form.

Georgia O'Keeffe was born in November 1887 in Sun Prairie, Wisconsin, and first studied art as a teenager at the Sacred Heart Academy in Madison. Though never a Catholic herself, she was fascinated with the religion's rituals and icons all her life—she would later paint many scenes of crosses in the Southwest—and some critics attributed mystical and "religious" elements in her paintings to this early association with Catholicism. O'Keeffe's real artistic roots, however, were firmly planted in Modernism and developed over an eight-year period in her twenties.

From 1907 to 1916, O'Keeffe worked with some of the most influential painter-teachers of her time, and studied modern art theory, in particular the psychology of color outlined in Wassily Kandinsky's *Concerning the Spiritual in Art*. Perhaps most importantly, she was introduced to the works of European and American artists at modernist exhibitions in New York—most notably those showcased at Alfred Stieglitz's 291 Gallery on Fifth Avenue. It was here that O'Keeffe's early charcoal abstractions were first exhibited in 1916, and where she met the renowned photographer and art patron who became her greatest champion, companion, and husband.

Artistically, O'Keeffe was greatly influenced by two men: William Merritt Chase, whose still-life classes she took at the Art Students League in New York in 1907, and the innovative art educator, Arthur Wesley Dow, with whom she studied composition for two years at Columbia Teachers College.

From Chase, a master of the still life who favored an orientalist approach to still-life composition, O'Keeffe learned the importance of studying a subject closely and intently. This respect for the "stilled form" would characterize all her work and is most dramatically evident in her large-scale still lifes of flowers, leaves, and shells. Yet she also brought the same intense, objective focus to her landscapes and abstractions, giving even a complex composition like *Summer Days* (plate 13), with its seemingly discordant mix of bones and flowers, a disturbing but "distinctive unity of effect."[3] It was with Chase that O'Keeffe also began to experiment with the power of color, later praising her teacher's "love of style—color—paint as paint. . . ."[4]

While O'Keeffe developed a personal approach to still-life composition radically different from Chase's more "classical" paintings, her *Horse-Red* (plate 2), an almost conventional design, painted with Seurat-like pointillist brushstrokes, is an early example of her experimentation with a vibrant and pure palette, a hearkening to Chase's "paint as paint." Later O'Keeffe still lifes, while bearing little compositional or stylistic resemblance to *Horse-Red*, were still elegant extenuations of the color lessons learned from Chase, as well as examples of his advice to find "a world of ideas" in a single object. *Alligator Pears in a Basket, No. 2* (plate 4) and *Apple Family III* (plate 5) garnered O'Keeffe critical acclaim in the early 1920s for their exceptional sense of color and innovative juxtapositions of rich but disparate hues. In these compositions, as well as in *Plums* (plate 17), painted during the same period, O'Keeffe also took the concept of the "stilled object" to new heights, embuing her fruits with such a celebratory organic pulse that they appear almost animated and "endowed with sentience . . . surrogates for human figures."[5]

In 1910, after a period of disillusionment with the art scene and a brief stint as a commerical artist in Chicago, O'Keeffe returned to Virginia where her family had moved eight years before. She taught briefly at the Chatham Institute, where she had attended high school, and then began taking art classes at the University of Virginia with Alon Bement, a former pupil of Arthur Wesley Dow and an ardent disciple of the Dow Method of composition, which O'Keeffe immediately embraced. From 1914 to 1916, while she taught summer classes in Virginia and Amarillo, Texas—her first introduction to the Southwest—O'Keeffe spent her winters studying with Dow in New York.

Like Chase, Dow stressed the importance of an "oriental aesthetic," but in particular, the Japanese concept of *notan*, where a painting is composed using balanced values of lights and darks.[6] In the early O'Keeffe abstracts, *Series I, No. 8* (plate 19), and especially *Series I, No. 4* (plate 30), so reminiscent of Hokusai's wave paintings, Dow's "orientalizing" influence is clearly evident. O'Keeffe would attribute Dow's measured but decorative approach to composition as the basis for her lifelong personal and professional compulsion to "fill a space in a beautiful way."[7]

Nowhere was Dow's influence more apparent than in O'Keeffe's flower paintings. In his art book, *Compositions*, Dow told students to paint, "not a picture of the flower . . . —that can be left to the botanist—but rather an irregular pattern of lines and spaces, something far beyond the mere drawing of a flower from nature."[8] Liberated by Dow's unique approach to art, O'Keeffe took the notion of going "beyond the mere drawing of a flower" to dazzling extremes. In her large floral designs of the 1920s, including *Abstraction White Rose II* (plate 8), *White Iris* (plate 26), *Two Calla Lillies on Pink* (plate 29), *Oriental Poppies* (front cover), and her series paintings of black irises, O'Keeffe not only catches the "stilled object"—canvases swimming with swirls of petals voluptuously curved, pulsating with color—but seems to "dive into" the very heart of the flower itself, pulling the viewer in with her. These astonishing designs, so different from the detailed, "realistic" still lifes produced only twenty years before, generated some of the most extraordinary art criticism of any time—and continue to do so. They have been variously interpreted as "morphological metaphors" for the female body, monuments to "the unity of the feminine and the natural order," or simply as "portraits of feminine states of feeling and mind."[9]

O'Keeffe always protested, to the end of her life, the more prurient interpretations of her large flower designs. Ever the pragmatist and formalist, she had this to say about her big paintings: ". . . nobody sees a flower—really—it is so small—we haven't time—and to see takes time. . . . So I said to myself—I'll paint what I see—what the flower is to me but I'll paint it big and they will be surprised into taking time to look at it—I will make even busy New Yorkers take time to see what I see of flowers.''[10] O'Keeffe also made people take time to ''see'' leaves and shells in her big paintings of those subjects. *The Broken Shell—Pink* (plate 28), painted ten years after her large floral compositions, continues her exploration of the aesthetic possibilities in rendering a single organic form as a dynamic whirl of flowing curves and counter-curves.[11]

From 1914 through the late 1920s, O'Keeffe's paintings are characterized largely by the artist's own ''looking inward'' and her experimentation with various techniques espoused by teachers, fellow painters, or suggested by her extensive readings. Kandinsky's inspired discussions of the power of color, particularly his psychological interpretations of red (as determined and powerful) and of blue (as spiritual and transcendent) greatly impressed O'Keeffe and when she turned from charcoal to color in 1916, blue became and remained her color of choice.[12] In an early color abstract, *Evening Star No. VI* (plate 3), one of a series of ten Evening Star watercolors, pure red and blue strokes are dramatically juxtaposed. In *Music—Pink and Blue II* (plate 9)—O'Keeffe's experiment with the technique of synaesthesia (translating the sensation of sound to the sensation of sight)—pale pink organic folds wrap around the central blue aperture, an expression of O'Keeffe's desire to create ''music that makes holes in the sky.''[13]

After O'Keeffe's marriage to Stieglitz in 1924, her artist's eye turned outward. During their residence in New York, O'Keeffe painted many Manhattan skyscapes, including her first Manhattan view, the haunting *New York with Moon* (plate 11). Summers and falls were spent at the Stieglitz family home in Lake George, New York, where evening sojourns by rowboat produced such studies as *Lake George Autumn* (plate 10).

O'Keeffe and Stieglitz had a powerful influence on one another, personally and professionally. Of him she said, "He would notice shapes and colors different from those I had seen and so delicate that I began to notice more." Of her effect on Stieglitz, a family associate said, "After Georgia came, he made the clouds, the moon, he even made lightning. He never photographed things like that before."[14] Their influence on each other's work can be seen in O'Keeffe's glorious *A Celebration* (plate 1), whose rolling clouds, vertical presentation, and blue and white colors echo Stieglitz's *Equivalent* series of photographic cloud studies, done during the same period.

Despite the couple's close relationship, O'Keeffe had a growing need to get away and work alone. She was increasingly drawn to the deserts of New Mexico, first spending winters there and, after Stieglitz's death in 1946, taking up permanent residence, first in Ghost Ranch, and later in Abiquiu.

O'Keeffe composed some of her greatest—and most mystifying works—from the dry white bones and relentless blue sky of the Southwestern desert. While some critics saw a morbid fascination with death in works like *Horse's Skull with Pink Rose* (plate 25), or ascribed an inscrutable and personal "symbolism" to the astonishing vision presented in *Ram's Head with Hollyhock* (plate 15), O'Keeffe maintained these paintings were as celebratory of life as her flowers. She was merely deriving inspiration from what nature now provided her—the detritus of the desert.

About her pelvis paintings, particularly the large-scale *Pelvis III* (plate 16), O'Keeffe put a most prosaic turn on these glimpses of sky through bone: "I was the sort of child that ate around the raisin in the cookie . . . the hole in the doughnut," she said, "saving the raisin or the hole for the last and best. . . . when I started painting the pelvis bones . . . they were most wonderful against the Blue—the Blue that will always be there after all men's destruction is finished . . . I have tried to paint the Bones and the Blue.''[15]

Georgia O'Keeffe died in 1986, at the age of ninety-nine. In her lifetime, she received unprecedented critical acclaim. She was elected to the National Institute of Arts & Letters, the American Academy of Arts & Letters, and received the United States Medal of Freedom. In 1946, she was the first woman honored with a retrospective at the Museum of Modern Art, and, twenty-five years later, the Whitney Museum's retrospective of this ''Mighty Mother's'' work garnered her renewed critical acclaim and an ardent feminist following. Before she began to lose her eyesight in the early 1970s, O'Keeffe was hurriedly completing her signature series of ''cloudscapes.'' *Sky Above Clouds II* (plate 32), painted when she was nearing 80, was one of her most ambitious projects, as innovative and astonishing as the charcoal abstracts that had hung in the 291 Gallery fifty years before. She was still creating ''things in my head that are not like what anyone has taught me.''

## NOTES

1. Anita Pollitzer, *A Woman on Paper: Georgia O'Keeffe* (New York: Simon & Schuster, Inc.), 238
2. Charles C. Eldredge, *Georgia O'Keeffe* (New York: Harry N. Abrams, Inc.), 17
3. Ibid, 59
4. Ibid
5. Ibid, 64–65
6. Ibid, 21
7. Ibid
8. Ibid, 75
9. Ibid, 88–89

10. Pollitzer, 226
11. Eldredge, 21
12. Ibid, 24
13. Ibid, 34
14. Ibid, 33, 49
15. Pollitzer, 239

# List of Plates

Photographs of art belonging to the Georgia O'Keeffe Foundation and private collections were supplied by Malcolm Varon, N.Y.C., © 1994, all others were supplied by:

FRONT
COVER
*Oriental Poppies*
Frederick R. Weisman Art Museum
at the University of Minnesota

BACK
COVER
*White Shell with Red Hills*
The Museum of Fine Arts, Houston
Gift of Isabel Wilson in memory of her mother,
Alice Pratt Brown

TITLE
PAGE
Laura Gilpin, *Georgia O'Keeffe* 1953
Copyright © 1994 Amon Carter Museum, Laura Gilpin
Collection

PLATE 1
*A Celebration*
© The Georgia O'Keeffe Foundation/
Artists Rights Society (ARS), New York

PLATE 2
*Horse-Red*
© The Georgia O'Keeffe Foundation/
Artists Rights Society (ARS), New York

PLATE 3
*Evening Star No. VI*
Private Collection
© The Georgia O'Keeffe Foundation/
Artists Rights Society (ARS), New York

PLATE 4
*Alligator Pears in a Basket, No. 2*
© The Georgia O'Keeffe Foundation/
Artists Rights Society (ARS), New York

PLATE 5
*Apple Family III*
© The Georgia O'Keeffe Foundation/
Artists Rights Society (ARS), New York

PLATE 6     *Corn, Dark II*
© The Georgia O'Keeffe Foundation/
Artists Rights Society (ARS), New York

PLATE 7     *Mountains and Lake*
© The Georgia O'Keeffe Foundation/
Artists Rights Society (ARS), New York

PLATE 8     *Abstraction White Rose II*
© The Georgia O'Keeffe Foundation/
Artists Rights Society (ARS), New York

PLATE 9     *Music—Pink and Blue II*
Collection of Whitney Museum of American Art, New York
Gift of Emily Fisher Landau in honor of Tom Armstrong

PLATE 10     *Lake George Autumn*
© The Georgia O'Keeffe Foundation/
Artists Rights Society (ARS), New York

PLATE 11     *New York with Moon*
Private Collection

PLATE 12     *Patio Door with Green Leaf*
© The Georgia O'Keeffe Foundation/
Artists Rights Society (ARS), New York

PLATE 13     *Summer Days*
Whitney Museum of American Art
Promised gift of Calvin Klein

PLATE 14     *Hills and Mesa to the West*
Private Collection

PLATE 15     *Ram's Head with Hollyhock*
Private Collection

PLATE 16     *Pelvis III*
Private Collection

PLATE 17     *Plums*
Private Collection

PLATE 18  *Bleeding Heart*
Private Collection

PLATE 19  *Series I, No. 8*
© The Georgia O'Keeffe Foundation/
Artists Rights Society (ARS), New York

PLATE 20  *The White Calico Flower*
Collection of Whitney Museum of American Art, New York

PLATE 21  *Series I, No. 2*
© The Georgia O'Keeffe Foundation/
Artists Rights Society (ARS), New York

PLATE 22  *Misti—A Memory*
© The Georgia O'Keeffe Foundation/
Artists Rights Society (ARS), New York

PLATE 23  *Dry Waterfall*
Collection of Emily Fisher Landau, New York

PLATE 24  *Horse's Skull with White Rose*
Private Collection

PLATE 25  *Horse's Skull with Pink Rose*
© The Georgia O'Keeffe Foundation/
Artists Rights Society (ARS), New York

PLATE 26  *White Iris*
Private Collection

PLATE 27  *Pink Sweet Peas*
Private Collection

PLATE 28  *The Broken Shell—Pink*
© The Georgia O'Keeffe Foundation/
Artists Rights Society (ARS), New York

PLATE 29  *Two Calla Lilies on Pink*
Philadelphia Museum of Art
Alfred Stieglitz Collection
Bequest of Georgia O'Keeffe

PLATE 30      *Series I, No. 4*
              © The Georgia O'Keeffe Foundation/
              Artists Rights Society (ARS), New York

PLATE 31      *Goat's Horn with Red*
              Hirshhorn Museum and Sculpture Garden
              Smithsonian Institution
              Gift of Joseph H. Hirshhorn, 1972
              Photographer, Lee Stalsworth

PLATE 32      *Sky Above Clouds II*
              Private Collection